A THERAPIST'S BASIC GUIDE TO WORKING WITH CHILDREN AND ADOLESCENTS

By Dr. Kristi B. Godwin, DPA, LMFT

"A Therapist's Basic Guide to Working with Children and Adolescents"

Published October 2018

BeTheAuthorOfYourLifeBook Publishing
Printed in the United States of America.

First Printing, United States, 2018

ISBN: 9781728775982

<u>Dedication:</u>

To the children and adolescents that I worked with during the first decade of my career. I carry a part of each of you with me still. You taught me how to be, what you needed and wanted, and in doing so it's really you who wrote this book. Thank you for the wisdom you imparted to me, and for every hug, smile, and sticker I received along the way!

"Although the world is full of suffering, it is also full of the overcoming of it."- Helen Keller

A Personal Note from the Author

Dear Reader,

I have always loved working with children and adolescents and preferred them to adult clients for the most part. Because of this I focused my clinical training efforts on courses that would aid me in working with the younger generations. I trained in play therapy, and many different therapy models with a specific focus on children and adolescents. Every training opportunity I had to hone my therapeutic skills I took advantage of. I simultaneously filtered my caseload to be comprised primarily of children and their families. I worked as an in-home therapist from 2007 until 2017, which means that most of the therapy sessions I conducted were with clients in their personal environments. I saw my clients in their schools during their school day, or at home with their families. I always sought to work with as much of the family system as possible, so my therapeutic work was in no way limited to children.

However, engaging the child as the primary client is a bit different than working exclusively with adults. I learned a few things along the way, and the purpose of this book is to share with you what I learned. If you are interested in working with children and adolescents, or are seeking to ease the joining process, I think this book may offer tips and insights to aid the journey for you. Best of luck to you in your work!

Warm regards,·

Kristi Godwin, LMFT

Table of Contents:

Chapter One:
Unconditional Positive Regard

Everyone has their own approach to therapy, including the "experts." That is why there are so many different therapeutic models to choose from! Which one is right, and which one is wrong? I personally believe there are effective and useful pieces to each theory, but that there is no ONE "right" theory out there. I have a quite eclectic approach myself, which I believe has served me very well thus far in my career. I use a variety of methods and basically customize each session to a degree, based on the individual client, their family system, and the issues currently at the forefront of the change lens in that moment. Maybe it would be easier to just ascribe to one particular model and apply it to every client I work with, but I personally find it much more challenging and even enjoyable to shift in the moment with my clients, as they need me to. It keeps me on my toes and continually pushes me to be my best.

With that in mind, I want to share with you one piece of several models that I find to be very important in forming a therapeutic relationship with a client. It is part of my therapeutic orientation that unconditional positive regard should be a basic tenant of every therapist-client relationship. My argument for that is that it fosters trust in the client for the therapist (also a necessary part of the relationship), and helps form a connection in which the client finds acceptance for who they are. I may not agree with everything Carl Rogers taught, but this is one part of his theory that I ascribe to. Unconditional positive regard refers to the acceptance and support of the therapist regardless of what the client says or does (Rogers 1980). Carl Rogers believed and proposed that mutual trust and respect are necessary for a healthy therapeutic relationship to engineer change (Rogers 1995). He also taught that congruence, unconditional positive regard, and empathic understanding are the three necessary core conditions of client-centered therapy (Rogers

1995). I absolutely agree and aspire to practice using empathetic and client-centered unconditional acceptance.

Children, in particular, need to feel loved, supported, and accepted in order to build the self-esteem, confidence, and security they require in order to effectively explore the world and develop their sense of self. From my personal experience, I can tell you that this is the secret ingredient to the best therapeutic alliances. This alone can overcome many presenting issues long enough to determine the root cause behind them and begin to initiate real change. With children, in particular, if you cannot overcome the presenting issue quickly, you will never have the opportunity to effect change. Let me give you an example of this:

A child presenting with oppositional defiance toward his teacher is referred to you for behavioral intervention. The complaints of the school and parents are that the child will not sit still for lessons, crumples up his assignments without completing them, throws a chair at the teacher who attempts to verbally redirect him, and runs from anyone attempting to address him directly. You are brought in to "fix" this issue. If you approach the child like the teachers, school staff, and even the parents have, the result will be the same. They approach with a stern face, a harsh, scolding tone of voice, sometimes aggressive body language, and toss around words like "defiant," "bad," "disruptive," and other negative terms. The child smiles and giggles and seems to view it as a game of tag, with the goal being to do the opposite of what he is being told and to deftly dodge any attempts to wrangle him in. And he appears to be very good at this game, by the way! Unconditional positive regard would dictate you approach the child with a smile, absent of concern, disappointment, or frown. You would simply eagerly and happily engage the child in conversation, or maybe play of some kind. And, in time, you would gently invite the child to play with you in another room. Once removed from the classroom you can express your positive regard for them more clearly, perhaps by complimenting him on how fast he can run, or by noticing some other positive trait from what you have observed. You begin to explain that you want to see him on a regular basis, and you have lots of fun things planned to do with him, and you offer a positive reward for his participation (depending on the age of the child…for

very young children I often used stickers). If he has difficulty sitting
you don't really pay attention, and you do not scold him for getting
up. You continue inviting him back to the seat, showing him
engaging activities you want him to join in on. This can take some
time, but after a few sessions (or a few weeks) you will no longer
have to invite him to sit. He won't run from you like he does the
other staff members, but will come toward you eagerly. He will ask
for you and look forward to sessions. And because he trusts you
after some time, he will begin to listen to your gentle suggestions,
and will even be willing to work hard to earn greater behavioral
rewards by being more compliant with classroom rules.

Anything less than unconditional positive regard will just result in more of the same, but that acceptance gains you his trust and his participation in therapy. A noncompliant client is one that is very difficult to change, I can tell you. If a child or an adult does not want to change, guess what?? They will not change! It's that simple. The most important thing you have to gain from any client in therapy is their willing participation. If you can't gain that then you are just wasting time.

Chapter Two:

The Joining Process

In order to gain a client's willing participation in therapy, it is essential to form a strong therapeutic alliance with the client. I recommend using unconditional positive regard as the foundation of your relationship; this foundation will be easy to build on in order to join. Go into the session viewing them in as positive a light as you can, regardless of their behavior or what you have been told about them. In my experience, oftentimes children are referred into therapy because of negative behaviors of some kind. The most common reasons for referrals I observed were defiance and attention issues. Attention deficit issues were the most common presenting issue I saw, second to that being oppositional defiance. In both of these cases, unfortunately, the child presented to me already "labeled" in a sense by school staff as "bad." I start off every session, and also most behavioral and parenting courses I teach, by making this statement, "I do not believe in bad children. I only believe in bad behavior." I think it is important to make that distinction for everyone involved, but the child definitely needs to know you are not defining them or viewing them as their behavior. The reality is that children act out their emotions because they do not know how to properly express them. They also act out what is modeled for them. Most of the time, disturbing behavior is there to call your attention to something very important that needs addressing. You are the detective in this mystery and it's your job to follow the behavioral clues to solve the mystery behind the behavior. Once you know the "answer," you can address it and resolve the issues.

Joining should come easily and naturally if you learn to follow these basic guidelines. As stated previously, always keep in mind unconditional positive regard. Meet the child or adolescent on their level. Get to know them, ask about their likes, dislikes, interests, hobbies, and respond positively regardless of what they share. Common interests are good to help connect you. For example, if their favorite color is the same as yours, say, "Oh, wow, that's my favorite color, too!" Or find common interests to discuss at length. Use the interests they have to build the relationship. If they like music, deliberately use musical interventions in therapy with them. If they enjoy art, be sure to use creative interventions with them. This lets them know you are paying attention and care what they like. This also helps foster trust and a connection and shows them that they can value and develop their own specific gifts, talents, and interests, and that you accept those things about them unconditionally.

Your undivided attention alone is very important. Many children do not receive undivided attention from anyone, not even their parent or guardian. Use active listening, and mirroring, as well-- expressing interest, empathy, and understanding while they are sharing with you. Ask questions to get to know them and to get them to open up about themselves. But be patient if they do not open up right away. Some children have deep betrayal wounds and are very hesitant to trust. I once waited patiently, giving unconditional acceptance to a young female client who would not answer any of my questions for over a year. My mouth nearly fell open in shock the day she finally decided to trust me and spontaneously opened up. She poured her thoughts and emotions out to me like a faucet suddenly turned on full-blast. But was completely silent for an entire year! That was the beginning of a wonderful therapeutic relationship that lasted several years. She is doing very well as an adult today, by the way! Be patient, be consistent, and be present with them regardless. Those are some of the biggest keys to joining with children.

Chapter Three:

Working With the System

Every child has their own unique system they live within. A system is defined as "a set of connected things or parts forming a complex whole," (Miriam-Webster 1999). When working with children it is vital that you also engage their systems. I recommend forming alliances with the school system, the teachers and staff that directly interact with the child, as well as their parents or guardians and other close family members. The child has limited agency for him or herself, and truly is largely a reflection of that system, so change is very restricted without everyone in the system on board.

The members of the system often hold valuable information (or clues) that you need in order to understand what is going on. The teachers spend a large amount of time daily with the child, as do the parents or guardians. You can enlist their help in looking for any kind of pattern around the troubling behaviors. Sometimes young children act out just because of an upset in routine....a new sibling, a recent move, a divorce, a change in the bedtime routine, or many other external factors. It is fairly common to see behavioral issues arise in a pattern that coincides with parental visitation when the parents are separated or divorced, for example. It is important to look for patterns, because it may require changes to be made at school and in the home in order to resolve the presenting issues. I always ask, "When did this issue first start? How often does it occur? What usually happens right before and right after the issue occurs? How do you normally address it?" And these questions may have different answers depending on who you ask, so it is important to ask this of the primary adult caretakers, including school or daycare staff, and guardians. It can be helpful to ask members of the system to keep a log over a period of a week or a few weeks tracking any associated facts or information, so they can be analyzed together in session later.

Another important thing to note is that you can only work with a child if you have the parent's permission. If you do not form and maintain a relationship with the family, or at least the primary guardian, then your work with the child could end before you are able to initiate change. Also, you will want to be able to potentially access the child in different environments, so it is important to have a good communicating relationship with the school, parents, and any other environment that they spend a great deal of time in. Children often behave differently in different environments, so seeing them in various settings will be very helpful for you in your work with them.

Oftentimes, a child's behavior directly coordinates with the parenting style of their guardian. Why would we think it is abnormal to have a small child scream obscenities at the teacher if we visit him or her at home and hear his or her parents doing the same to them? Again, children will model what they see and hear. We must always keep in mind the context of the situation and be familiar with what is "normal" for the child. This absolutely varies from child to child. I was astounded when I first began working with children to see just how vast these variations can be. It is also not uncommon for one of the primary interventions when working with a child to be to employ some parental teaching. Parents are also modeling what was taught to them, and if they do not know better they cannot do better. Sometimes psychoeducation helps, sometimes it doesn't. But be prepared to utilize that at times, because you will most likely need to. When a child is repeatedly exposed to specific behaviors, we cannot expect them to do otherwise. Therapy, in such cases, is almost useless until the child is older. In working with older children, you can begin to have conversations with them around this. *"Just because mom and dad do/say xyz does not mean it is appropriate. If your teacher will give you detention for xyz, then you have to decide what is the best choice of behavior for YOU."* They can begin to have more agency over themselves and try to break some of the patterns set before them. They can logically decide who they want to be as a person, rather than just repeat learned behaviors. Being aware of the system they operate in is still important, though. The more information you have about the client the better you are able to help them.

Chapter Four:
The Art of Creativity

I personally find that using art in therapy is a great way to break down invisible walls and help people to be more emotionally vulnerable. I use art therapy with many of my clients, regardless of their age. I always used art at least some when working with children and adolescents. With very young children who are not entirely verbal, art and play therapy are the primary ways to both gain information from them and to express information to them. I will explain more about using play therapy in session later, but for now I will focus on art. Most children enjoy coloring, drawing, and even painting. I kept on hand watercolor paints, watercolor paper, drawing paper, colored pencils, crayons, and colored markers to have available as needed. I would often ask a client to draw themselves, and to draw their families. How a child or adolescent depicts their family in a drawing can be very telling. They reveal far more than they mean to most of the time. If a child has difficulty telling me how they feel, I often ask them if they can draw it out. If something has happened, for instance they have been exposed to something traumatic, I may ask them to draw what they saw. I have seen 3-year-olds clearly depict natural disasters, sexual abuse, and domestic violence in their drawings. They may not know how to verbalize it, but they can sketch it out roughly.

Anything you want to know from a child, or even a teenager, you can ask them to draw. Sometimes it is easier for them to depict it than it is to formulate the words and speak it out loud. If they are holding secrets (such as abuse), they can show you what they are not allowed to say to you. Art really is a very effective tool in that way. Art is also very therapeutic…just the act of creating something original, something new, unique, and beyond words, is an outlet for pent up emotion, or emotion not yet understood. There are many ways to use art in therapy, so I encourage you to use your imagination and be as creative as you can be. I will share a few of the ways I used art with you…feel free to do something completely different, or to alter these in any way to make them your own:

Painting Your Nails Drawing Activity:

Have them trace their hand and draw on fingernails, then they can color in the nails and decorate them. Ask them to choose colors to represent the emotions they are feeling, and to paint their nails with those colors. As they color have them explain what the colors represent to them. Ask what things cause them to feel that.

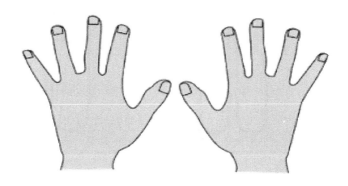

Color Your Emotion Activity:

Have them fill in the emotion key to indicate which colors represent what emotion, and have them color in the person to illustrate how much of each emotion they feel, and if they feel it in a particular part of their body.

Emotion Key:

Color: **Emotion:**

Draw Your Family Activity

This activity is especially helpful for really young children, ages 3 to 10. But even older children can reveal a great deal of information in a quick family sketch. Don't give any specific instructions other than "Will you draw a picture of your family for me?" You can also ask for a picture of their house and family. Either are helpful, both together are best. There are things to look for in the drawing that will help you understand. Notice the distance between the people, how they are positioned, their sizes relative to each other, whether their faces are happy or sad, or neither, and what they appear to be doing in the drawing. Notice if there are other people outside of the family present, if there are pets included, or objects, and particularly notice the child and how and where they positioned themselves. What you are seeing is how they view themselves and their position in their family. Feel free to ask questions of them as they draw, and about the picture they drew. If you are not sure who the individuals depicted are, ask. I usually ask them to label the individuals, or if they are not able to I label them for them. This is useful for studying the picture after the session has ended.

There are lots of books and scholarly articles on the interpretation of drawings if you care to study the specifics. I would suggest not jumping to radical conclusions without doing some research first, but also using your basic therapeutic skills to interpret what your clients present to you.

Past and Future Hands

(Original idea found on Pinterest)

This is a fun and simple activity that challenges clients to self-reflect and confront their own need to change. This is best used in older children (8 and above), and also works great for adults. Give them a blank piece of paper and ask them to trace both hands. Their left hand represents their past, and their right hand represents their future. Ask them to fill their left hand up with things they want to leave in their past, things they want to overcome, or things they want to resolve and be free of. Ask them to then fill their right hand with things they want to achieve, personal goals, and things they want to have in their future. They are allowed to use words, symbols, and images to depict these things in their hands. Most people use a combination of these. I've posted an example of this below:

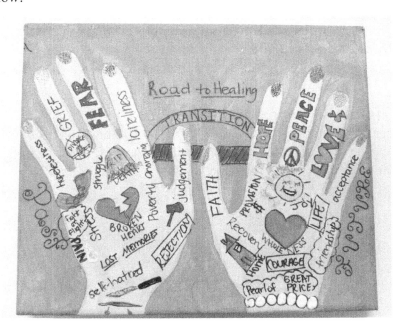

Chapter Five:
Let's Play a Game!

I highly recommend the use of games when working with children. Most children respond positively to games, and it is an incredible tool for bonding. The game tends to distract them so that you can ask questions to gather information and they may be more forthcoming than is typical. There are plenty of games out there developed especially for therapy but they can be expensive. I personally think any game can be used therapeutically. The game of Life, in particular, is great for future planning and life skill building when working with older children and adolescents. I find Uno to be an easy disarming tool to use, also. It's a simple game most children can learn and follow easily and doesn't require so much concentration that they are unable to simultaneously have a conversation with you. I have also found that many kids enjoy Jenga, and there is an easy therapeutic twist if you care to put in a little more effort. You can write questions (or glue/tape typed questions) on the Jenga blocks for the clients to answer as they pull the blocks out. Lists of therapeutic questions can be found on Pinterest or online if you have trouble thinking of your own. Monopoly is a great game to help them learn strategy, business development, and financial planning.

When working with preschoolers and elementary age children I also have used the battery-operated fishing game. The younger children particularly enjoy catching the fish while we talk. There are many card games to use, as well. Go Fish, War, and Crazy Eights are a few I have used. For preschool children I also use a match game to help them learn to take turns and control their impulses. Games are great for impulse control and also for emotional control when they are not doing well or lose a game. Using games in therapy also helps foster the idea that therapy is FUN….you want the kids to look forward to your sessions, not dread them. The use of games is a good way to engage them and facilitate the joining process in the first few sessions.

Using creative therapy with teenagers helps keep them engaged and active in therapy. Some activities you can use to engage them in the therapeutic process are: Jenga, card games, board games, ball games (play catch with them using a small bean bag or stress ball….each time they throw the ball they have to answer a question), art activities, goal worksheets, collages (have them do one about themselves, one for their goals, one to represent their family, etc.), have them scrapbook or keep an art journal, and ask them to rewrite their favorite songs to represent themselves in a positive way. Again, it's really about using what you know they love in a therapeutic way…. the sky is the limit!

Chapter Six:
Using Play Therapy Techniques

The beauty of play therapy is that ANYTHING can be used therapeutically. Play therapy is really just being creative in using material objects to engage in play in a therapeutic way. It is learning how to gather information through play and learning how to initiate change through play. If you work with children, I highly encourage you to attend a play therapy conference. Play therapy was an essential part of my work with children. It helped me join with them, it helped me communicate with them, and I really do not think I could have done any sort of effective therapy with the younger children without it. Older children who can effectively communicate their feelings and thoughts are totally different from three and four-year-olds who are barely verbal. I worked with the whole spectrum!

I used play therapy not just with children but with individual adults and families, as well. I still use play therapy even though I now work in an inpatient setting exclusively with adult women. You won't regret the training, that I am sure of.

Play therapy encompasses so many things that I will not attempt to cover them all here. I am going to limit this tremendously to a few of my favorite techniques. Please keep in mind this guide is just one therapist sharing tips with another, and I am not trying to "train" anyone in any particular therapeutic model. Many play therapists use sand trays, and it is possible to make a very functional portable sand tray for therapists that travel, as I did. I did not do that, but I believe it is a very useful tool if you care to explore the use of sand in therapy. My practice generally focused on the use of small toys, dolls, puppets, games, books, and play doh. I found a reasonably priced set of small animal finger puppets and would allow my clients to choose one or two for a session. They could talk through their puppet and I would talk through mine. Having the puppet express things is much easier for children to do than express them directly.

I also would allow them to show me their normal home routines using dolls or figures. I would ask them to choose a doll or figure to represent the primary people in their household, and to show me what a normal day looked like. I would ask them to show me bedtime routines, mealtimes, play time, etc. Children tend to be very expressive and quite a bit of information can come through this way. Unfortunately, sometimes very unpleasant information that is heartbreaking will be revealed this way. Still, all the information you get is useful for you.

Play doh is something that most children love. In fact, most of the children I worked with would request it each week and some would not want to do anything but play with the play doh. I would usually teach them how to sculpt some simple things with the play doh (this builds a sense of accomplishment in them, and also helps them learn how to use the play doh to create anything they want to). I would show them how to flatten the doh, how to create a ball with it, how to make a pizza and add their own toppings, how to roll it out into a snake, and how to roll the snake into a snail. This is very easy to do even for a novice. Even three-year-olds are able to do these things and they have such a sense of pride from it! Once we do these things a few times I ask them to make whatever they want to. Older children or children with good motor skills can go so far as to make a tea set with the play doh, complete with cookies and cakes for the party, or trucks, trains, and tractors. There is no limit to what can be made once you learn how to make basic shapes. The play doh serves to build self-esteem, develop motor skills, allow them to create and show you things they may not be able to express verbally, and also to distract them from the fact that you are doing therapy. They will chatter away while they sculpt!

Play therapy involves the use of symbolism. Toys and other play items are wonderful representatives for therapeutic use. For example:

- Plastic dinosaurs can represent "monsters" (abusers, bullies, enemies, "the dark", etc)

- Toy animals (and more obviously, dolls) can represent family members

- Plastic animals can be used to represent both strengths and weaknesses

- Blocks can be used to represent obstacles, goals, and many life principles

- Colors (crayons, markers, cards) can be used to represent emotions

Any type of small toy can be used, such as matchbox cars or plastic dinosaurs or other animals. You ask the child to choose one and then ask them why they chose that particular one. You can also ask them which one most represents who they are, or members of their family, and why. You can race cars with them, or conduct role plays with the plastic animals. An example of using small animals would be the following scenario:

Therapist: *Johnny, which of these animals do you think is most like you? Or which one would you be if you could be?*

Johnny: *I think the lion.*

Therapist: *Why the lion? What qualities does the lion have that you have, too? Or what qualities does the lion have that you want to have?*

Johnny: *Lions are strong and powerful, and I want to be powerful like that. Lions are also brave. I wish I could be brave and* *strong and powerful because Billy wouldn't pick on me anymore if I was.*

Therapist: *Bravery or courage actually doesn't mean you aren't afraid anymore. Bravery just means that you push past your fear and do what you should do anyway. If you were a lion what would you say or do to Billy?*

Of course, not every interaction with play therapy will be that direct, but that's an example of how you could use a plastic animal to engage in therapy with a young child.

The other thing I used often with children is books. I kept a few books on hand that involved the defining of emotion. I believe an important part of therapeutic work with children is gauging and developing their emotional intelligence. Using books is a great way to help them understand different emotions so that you can more easily discuss and process emotions in sessions. I also kept on hand books to help develop impulse control. Poor impulse control was something I saw often in the children I worked with, either due to attention deficit issues, anger issues, or defiance issues. Regardless, I found that the use of books that were interactive in some way helped them develop better impulse control. I found a few books that had a button that made a noise when pressed, and on each page there was an opportunity for the button to be pressed. I would instruct the client during the first session that they could have the privilege of helping me with the book by pressing the button when prompted. This first session would be my baseline for them….if they could not wait for the prompts then I knew their impulse control was very poor, and the better they were able to resist the urge to press the button is the more progress I knew we had made. This worked very well for children aged 2 to 7. I also tried to keep on hand books dealing with some of the more common therapeutic issues, such as divorce, grief, compliance with rules, anger, and impulse control, and I would read these or have them read them to me when appropriate.

Chapter Seven:
Building and Using a Therapy Kit

When I first was trained in play therapy I developed a play therapy kit (which I transported easily in a large shoulder bag) that I kept on hand at all times. I highly recommend you do this if you work with children. Some of the things I kept in my play therapy bag are:

- a pack of Uno cards

- a pack of regular playing cards

- a small Ziploc bag of matchbox cars

- a small Ziploc bag of plastic animals

- a pack of crayons

- a pack of markers

- a pack of colored pencils

- art paper

- a Ziploc bag of small dolls (preferably a "family"…an adult male, and an adult female, and at least one boy child and one girl child)

- a Ziploc bag of assorted finger puppets

- a small tin of dominos

- a Jenga game

- at least a few containers of play doh (different colors)

- assorted children's books (at least one of which is interactive)

- a few different age-level puzzles

- an assorted pack of rubber bands (CBT/DBT)

- cotton balls

- assorted essential oil scents (peppermint, eucalyptus, lemon, orange, lavender)

- an assortment of stickers

I was able to get these items from a local dollar store at very reasonable prices, with the exception of the puppets and dolls, which I found at a local hobby store. Play therapy does not require a huge financial investment, but purchasing a few strategic items can make an incredible difference in your effectiveness in therapy.

I consider these items to be pretty basic. I used them all on a regular basis. There were times when I had other items, as well, and times when I wished I had much more, but you can function well as a therapist with just these items. At one point I did carry around a small doll house, complete with furniture. This was quite useful as it allowed the kids to show me their home life pretty accurately. However, it was a little bulky and difficult to transport from place to place and eventually I discarded it. I had a magnetic house with figures and furniture I carried with me, as well, but eventually the pieces went missing and I discarded that. There is no limit to what you can obtain to use, it just depends on your creativity, your willingness to invest, and what you are willing to carry around with you (provided you do in-home, or in-school, therapy like I did). Ideally, having a play therapy space in your fixed office would be best, and you could have a sand tray, a water table, and anything else your play therapist heart can dream of! For now, though, decide what is practical for you in your practice and customize it to that.

A First Session with a Young Child

When working with children ten and under, my first session would consist of an informal assessment of their fine motor skills, their language skills, and their mental age. I would introduce myself as Ms. Kristi and explain to them that I would like to start spending time with them once a week. I would show them some of the items in my play therapy bag and tell them they will get to choose a sticker each time they allow me to spend time with them and cooperate with the tasks I ask them to complete. I would then ask if they would try some things for me. The vast majority of the time I received complete cooperation at this point, but if I received any resistance I would not push or scold, but I might say, "Well, maybe you will want to do some of these things the next time I visit. It has been very nice meeting you. Thank you for talking with me. Would you like a sticker today for spending a few minutes with me?" And then I would end the session. If they are willing to proceed, I would take out about five or six of the dominoes and ask them to watch without moving. I would ask them to be very still. This is to test their impulse control and ability to follow directions, primarily. I would then line the dominoes up in a row, standing on the ends. I would pause dramatically (giving them the opportunity to upset the dominoes), and then ask them to watch my "magic trick" as I gently tap the first domino in the line, and we both would watch the dominoes tumble down the line. Next, I would line them up again the same way, but I would ask them would they like to be the one to knock them down this time. This increases the difficulty of resisting the impulse for them. They typically are very eager to knock down the dominoes and sometimes cannot let me complete the line first. I ask them initially to wait until I instruct them to, but some children are not able to wait. This gives me a good baseline for their impulse control either way. I then let them knock down the dominoes. Last, I ask them to try to line up the dominoes as I have, and knock them down without my help. This gives me a good idea of their fine motor skills and their ability to concentrate. This can sometimes be very difficult for three and four-year-olds, but most are able to do it after a few tries. Older children should definitely have the ability to do this and any difficulty could indicate a delay or another issue.

I then take out the play doh. I give them a small amount and I take a small amount. I ask them to try to copy me as I roll the dough into a ball.

I then flatten the dough into a flat circular shape, like a pancake.

If they have difficulty I slow down and instruct more or help them with theirs if necessary. Again, this is all giving me information about the child and what their abilities are. I can easily see if they have used play doh before or if this is foreign to them. I then reform a ball out of the play doh and start to roll it out into a long rope like piece. As I roll I ask if they know what we are making. Sometimes they guess correctly and sometimes they do not know. We make a snake like this, and form a small head. I let them take my pen and make eyes on their snake's head. I offer to let them play with the snake, which most want to do. They slither around and I ask what do snakes do? What sounds do they make? And just make general conversation with them as they play.

When they seem to be getting bored with the snake I ask them if I can I show them another trick. I then show them how to start with the snake's tail and roll the snake body up into a coil all the way up to the head, but leaving the head out. This makes a snail.

Sometimes they say, "Oh, we made Gary!" They are referring to the pet snail on the SpongeBob cartoon.

I agree with them if they say this. It is really good if you can use any language they present, and also bring in their favorite familiar book and television characters. I often would try to create out of play doh a character if I knew what their favorites were. I would ask, "What would you like us to make today?" and we create whatever they dream up as best we can. This definitely aids in joining as it shows the child you are paying attention, and you care about what they like. I then give them a few minutes to free-play with the play doh.

When ready, I move on to the Draw-A-Family activity. I put a blank piece of paper before them and get out the crayons and colored pencils, or maybe the markers. I ask them if they can try to draw a picture of themselves with their family. I give them time to do this, but I may ask questions as they go. I may ask them to label the individuals in their drawing, or if they are very young I will ask if I can label the people so I can remember who they are. I will ask, "Now, who is that you just drew?" and I will write the name they give next to the figure in the drawing. After they finish I may go back and re-name the individuals verbally with them to make sure that I have it labeled correctly. I may also ask why they drew things a specific way. "I see that you are off in one corner of the paper, and your mom is over in the other corner. Why does she seem so far away from you?" Or "I see that your sister is smiling in the picture, but you do not look very happy. Why aren't you smiling in the picture?" This just gives me even more information about them. I always keep these drawings to look at after the session ends to make sure I didn't miss anything important.

I will then pull out an interactive book to do a test of their attention span and further test their impulse control. I will explain to them the rules of the book…I will read the book and they are to be the "button masher" assistant, but they can only press the button when prompted. This is an excellent determinant of the baseline of their attention span and impulse control. I will easily be able to tell if they are improving from session to session simply by doing this exercise during each session, or at regular intervals. They love doing this, and sometimes will actually start doing the reading for me, as well, after a few sessions. That is fine, also. The point is to keep their attention for the span of the book, and to have them wait until prompted to press any buttons. After completing this activity, I will thank them for being so willing to talk with me and ask if it is okay for me to come and see them again (I always got a yes to that question!). I will explain that I will be coming to see them once per week and I will always bring fun things to do, and if they do the activities with me they will always get a sticker at the end. I then let them choose a sticker from my sticker stash and return them to class or to their mother.

A First Session with A Child Over Ten

With an older child my approach may be completely different depending on their mental age. Some older children may be autistic or may have some mental disabilities. If a child's mental age is under ten even though they are biologically ten or older, I will still begin with the same routine I use for younger children. Always try to keep your session age-appropriate. The same goes for a younger child who is very mature for their age. I have worked with four-year-olds who were mentally closer to ten or eleven. For those children I would adopt my older techniques even though they are only four. It usually takes an initial session or two to figure out that they are that advanced, though, so you could still start with the younger protocol, just know that it is absolutely fine to customize your session to each child depending on their particular level.

With an older child I would do much more conversation and less activity. I may start out with the Draw-A-Family activity because the way they draw out individual figures will give me a good idea of their mental age and will give me helpful information about their family make-up. I will be asking questions as they draw and may also ask them unrelated questions as they draw. "What kinds of things do you like to do?" "What's your favorite color?" "What kinds of music do you like?" "What's your favorite movie?"

"What's your favorite subject in school?" Or other "getting to know you" questions. I customize future sessions to their likes and dislikes as much as I can. If they are super-into origami, guess what we will be doing in the next session? Yep! You guessed it—origami! I think flexibility and willingness to try new things is also important when working with children. Get your boots on and get ready to get dirty!

After they complete the drawing activity and I have the information I need about that, I will pull out the Jenga game. If they do not want to play Jenga or seem to have great difficulty playing it (it does require some mental strategy as well as dexterity) then I would revert to using the therapeutic questions taped to the blocks while I let them build random things with the blocks. They can build a house, a tower, or whatever they want to. As they work we talk. If they seem disinterested in this, I may pull out the Uno game instead. Or the play doh. Kids of all ages seem to enjoy the play doh. Even the adults I work with love making things with it. No age limits! At the end of the session you can offer a sticker (some kids love those well into the teen years). Many older kids no longer need a reward, just having your attention is reward enough for them. I tended to use behavioral rewards more with the older kids as incentives to improve behavior over longer periods of time rather than each session. You can do this however you would like to, though!

So, for the older kids you will continue using play therapy techniques with things in your bag, but you will be better able to converse and gain information as you play than with the younger kids. Younger children tend to be far less verbal and you will get the majority of your information from their play, whereas older kids can more easily verbalize to you their emotions, thoughts, and issues, but will relax more and perhaps reveal additional information through drawings and play. Make sense? I hope so! That's it in a nutshell!

Chapter Eight:

It Takes a Village to Raise a Child

Part of your job as a therapist working with children will be to stay aware of community resources. You will need to gauge the family system and the child's needs. How well is the family meeting their needs? Are the parents overwhelmed and unable to meet the needs of the child? You can make gentle recommendations for outside resources where appropriate. Getting the child involved in extracurricular activities, after school programs, tutoring programs, special needs assistance, a mentoring program, or even making a referral to the local child services agency are all things to keep in mind.

As a therapist you are a mandated reporter, which means that you are required to report suspected abuse of any kind. The wellbeing of the child is always the most important thing. If you encounter a situation you feel needs to be reported, it is best to try to salvage the therapeutic relationship with the child and family if at all possible. You can try to address the situation directly with the guardians and let them be a part of the reporting process. If it is possible the child(ren) may be removed from the home, collaborate with the family to determine if there are other relatives who can take guardianship to keep the children from going into state custody. If you do not feel this is wise, or safe, but still hope to continue to work with the family and want your alliance to stay intact, another option to explore is having other involved parties (such as teachers, school staff, doctors, or other mandated professionals) who you have spoken with about your concerns make the report. For example, I often had a teacher bring their concerns to me to explore with the client. When the client divulged confirmation of the suspected abuse I would not directly report immediately, but would first ask the teacher I had already spoken with to report. I would not give her confidential information but would just tell her I also believe there is reason for concern and a report needs to be made. I would ask if she is comfortable making the report. If so, I would then ask her to also be sure to give the agency my name and number so that I can give them the appropriate information and be kept informed of the investigation and its findings. When this was feasible, I was able to remain an involved party with a strong alliance with the family and could help them navigate the whole process. At times I was able to continue working with the children even after they were removed from the home. Unfortunately, when I myself made the report, it always interfered with my therapeutic relationship in the long run. In the end, you will have to make the judgement call for each situation you encounter, but exploring different options is sometimes very helpful for the overall wellbeing of the child.

If the child seems to need something the family is not able to provide, consider what local resources may be helpful for them. It may not be uncommon for the children you work with to be under the guardianship of a family member and not with a biological parent, or to be in a single-parent home. These situations may include extra financial strain or overwhelming stress, but the families may not be aware of what resources they have available. This is something to always be conscious of and to assist in when you can.

Chapter Nine:

Incorporating Various Therapeutic Models

You can adapt and incorporate any model you are trained in for children, so don't panic. However, I will share here the leading models recommended by professionals based on research, as well as the models that I personally found to be the most helpful in my work. Most of my work was based in the following therapeutic models:

Cognitive Behavioral Therapy

Dialectical Behavior Therapy

Play Therapy

Narrative Therapy

Solution Focused Therapy

Family Systems Theory

Structural Therapy

Eye Movement Desensitization and Reprocessing (EMDR)

I did not personally conduct research on these models, so my opinions are solely that, my OPINIONS based on my personal education and experience as a therapist. I did receive training in all of the aforementioned models, so it was easy for me to incorporate those into my work. Those were the models that seemed to come most naturally to me as I worked, and the ones I found to be most effective over the years. I did receive training in other models, but these are the ones I primarily used. This may solely be due to my personality and personal preferences and may be totally unrelated to their stand-alone effectiveness in therapy. Because I am acknowledging my own biases, I will also include information on the models shown through years of research to be effective in work with children and adolescents.

I will briefly outline how I used each of these models in my work. CBT was the primary mode of therapy used for very young children as I used rewards to motivate behavioral changes and repetitive activities in therapy to build various skillsets. I used some cognitive psychoeducational training with the parents and teachers, as well as the children, around various diagnoses and behaviors. My intention out of graduate school was not to use this particular model, but I quickly learned that it was effective and efficient, and just made the most sense given the setting and population I worked with.

DBT was the primary mode of therapy I used with older children, and I taught some of the self-soothing skills as well as mindfulness to all children, regardless of age. Mindfulness generally helps increase the attention span as well as decrease hyperactivity. To incorporate mindfulness with children, here are a few things you can do:

- Have them sit with eyes closed and LISTEN. After a time have them report what they have heard and what they know based on those sounds (inside or outside activity)

- Have them practice focusing on ONE THING and noticing all details of that one thing (using all senses…the one thing can be a favorite toy or just something nearby)

- Do a mindfulness activity using a piece of candy, raisin, or other edible item (see ONE RAISEN activity in the appendix)

- Have them practice mindfulness as you walk around or participate in any activity

DBT includes some incredible skillsets to build impulse control. These skills can help adolescents and teens navigate emotional ups and downs related to life changes, anger, heartbreak, or self-harm impulses. I taught these skillsets to any client I had that struggled at all with anger management, depression and anxiety, suicidality, or self-harm behaviors, and the majority of my older children fit into those categories. I used the five senses for self-soothing and carried items in my therapy kit for the teaching of five senses (see the appendix). I used essential oils for scent, peppermint or junior mints for taste, silk or cotton for touch, and a nature video for both sight and hearing (easily pulled up on my smart phone). The five senses for self-soothing works wonderfully for all ages, even adults. It is easy to learn and easy to put into practice as needed.

I was able to use a fair amount of narrative therapy with the older children and teens. In the initial sessions you can get a good feel for how intellectual and logical a child is. If they were capable of accepting reframes and metaphorical language, I always used it. Even some of the very young children were able to grasp this on a more elementary level, but primarily this was a useful tool with the older teens.

As I mentioned earlier, I used play therapy with all ages to different degrees. I still use play therapy today in my work with adult women. I highly recommend play therapy training, particularly if you work with children primarily.

Two foundations for my work, even beneath the other mentioned modalities, is the understanding of family systems theory and the drive to be solution focused. I suppose you could say those were woven throughout the other therapy modalities in my use of them. Family systems was vital in working with the school and family systems of the children, so I used it to some degree with every case I ever had. Family systems theory was really the lens through which I saw everything I encountered.

I also used some structural therapy. This was only used when working with multiple family members (or members of a system). I always noted the way the different family members positioned themselves in the room, their body language and the hierarchal operation of the family overall. I would sometimes use family sculpturing and role plays among family members when working with families, as well.

I was able to use EMDR's negative and positive cognitions to get to the root of issues with clients, and with children could use eye movements, tapping, or stomping for bilateral brain stimulation to work through difficult memories or past traumas in order to reduce the negative emotions and beliefs attached to those memories.

The Society of Clinical Child and Adolescent Psychology lists the following modalities as evidence-based therapies for children and adolescents (2018):

- Applied Behavior Analysis

- Behavior Therapy

- Cognitive Behavior Therapy

- Cognitive Therapy

- Family Therapy

- Interpersonal Psychotherapy

- Organization Training

Their website (https://effectivechildtherapy.org/therapies/) gives an explanation of these various modalities, as well as brief informational videos (courtesy Cynthia Hartung, PhD from the University of Wyoming). I will include links to those below if you have an interest in learning more:

Modular Cognitive-Behavioral Therapy for Childhood Anxiety by Lauren Zimmerman & Angeline Bottera
https://www.youtube.com/watch?v=1TcTNz4IvXE

Multifamily Psychoeducational Psychotherapy for Childhood Bipolar Spectrum Disorders

by Kandice Perry & Katy Richardson

https://www.youtube.com/watch?v=ZBDPMohZqeY&t=3s

Trauma-Focused Cognitive-Behavioral Therapy for Children & Adolescents

by Kati Lear & Sarah Steinmetz

https://www.youtube.com/watch?v=JTcjMPoxUTM

Cognitive-Behavioral Therapy for Adolescent Depression

by Brooke Maxfield & Kendal Binion

https://www.youtube.com/watch?v=VXJy0X0OZtI

Hyperactivity Disorder

by Christopher Shelton & Ryan Kozina

https://www.youtube.com/watch?v=IVG4SWEZCT4

Coping Cat to Treat Anxiety in Children and Adolescents

by Andrea Slosser & Shira Kern

https://www.youtube.com/watch?v=qE5QpJ_FaJ8

Parent Management Training for Childhood Behavior Problems

by Adam Ripley & Alejandra Reyna

https://www.youtube.com/watch?v=YMl8cKe9DD0

There is a vast wealth of information out there on various techniques and therapeutic modalities for working with children. My goal in this book is not to give an exhaustive list of these but to give you a brief synopsis of the techniques I found most useful. I hope to give you a jumpstart or maybe a fresh view of work with children, but I invite you to educate yourself further as you feel led. I may even recommend starting the work and figuring out what additional training you need as you go along. Depending on your own style you will sense what areas you need to develop, I think.

Chapter Ten:

Know Your Limitations

Knowing your limitations as a therapist is very important. You are still human, after all. Many things can affect your ability to be therapeutic with your clients. Children can equally be energizing and draining, so I think it may be particularly important to be attentive to your own needs when working with children. Know the limits of a healthy caseload for you. Don't overload yourself, all of your kids will suffer. And so will you!

Make sure to always incorporate some self-care. Have a therapist yourself, be in supervision, have colleagues or supervisors to talk over your cases with, and take time to just relax and do things you enjoy. And when you encounter a very difficult case that emotionally drains you, do not hesitate to take a mental health break. I have some cases that still haunt me to this day. I would stay awake nights worrying about cases and agonize over them long after therapy ended. Don't do that! Learn from my mistakes and draw healthy boundaries for yourself. Understand going in that you will not be able to help every child, and you have no control over their situations, really. You can only do what you can do. And you have to make peace with the final outcome.

The hardest cases for me have been the ones I have had to make reports on. It has never ended well for me. I lose my therapeutic relationship with the clients once the report has been made and then they disappear into the system and I am left wondering if the kids are okay or not. It is not a good feeling. I am hesitant to report, and I make every effort to address the concerns with the parents or guardians before reporting, but sometimes that just is not possible. Sometimes the children are at too much risk to try to address it yourself. Those are the ones I lose sleep over.

I won't go into too much detail on the horror stories I have seen, but just hear my warning and try to know your limitations and have a plan for how to take care of yourself in the event that something like that happens. Incorporate deliberate self-care into your weekly schedule and have a supportive team of professionals around you in your work. Never be afraid to ask for help, clinical advice, or vent when you become frustrated over a case. All therapists experience those things from time to time. Remember that you need to oxygenate yourself before you can help others! Above all, embrace the motto that started me in this field: if you only help ONE CHILD, then it is all worth it! But I am sure you will help many more than one!

Appendix:

Formal Practice: Mindfully Eating a Raisin

Place a few raisins in your hand. If you don't have raisins, any food will do. Imagine that you have just come to Earth from a distant planet without such food.

Now, with this food in hand, you can begin to explore it with all of your senses.

Focus on one of the objects as if you've never seen anything like it before. Focus on seeing this object. Scan it, exploring every part of it, as if you've never seen such a thing before. Turn it around with your fingers and notice what color it is.

Notice the folds and where the surface reflects light or becomes darker.

Next, explore the texture, feeling any softness, hardness, coarseness, or smoothness.

While you're doing this, if thoughts arise such as "Why am I doing this weird exercise?" "How will this ever help me?" or "I hate these objects," then just see if you can acknowledge these thoughts, let them be, and then bring your awareness back to the object.

Take the object beneath your nose and carefully notice the smell of it.

Bring the object to one ear, squeeze it, roll it around, and hear if there is any sound coming from it.

Begin to slowly take the object to your mouth, noticing how the arm knows exactly where to go and perhaps becoming aware of your mouth-watering consistency as you chew.

When you feel ready to swallow, consciously notice the intention to swallow, then see if you can notice the sensations of swallowing the raisin, sensing it moving down to your throat and into your esophagus on its way to your stomach.

Take a moment to congratulate yourself for taking this time to experience mindful eating.

Clark, G. (2015). Mindfully Eating a Raisin. Retrieved August 5, 2015, from http://www.mbsrtraining.com/mindfully-eating-a-raisin-exercise/

DISTRESS TOLERANCE
Using Crisis Survival: Distraction with Wise Mind Accepts

A Activities—engage in activities that require concentration
C Contributing—look for a way to help others around you
C Comparisons—remember to be grateful for what you have
E Emotions--find something to shift you into the opposite emotion
P Pushing Away—walk away, push it away, or mentally leave
T Thoughts—find something to focus your thoughts on
S Sensations—use a physical sensation to shock you out it

Using Self Soothe with the five senses:

- Taste—use a soothing or distracting taste to calm you
- Smell—use a pleasant, calming scent to soothe you
- See—use a comforting, relaxing, or joyous image
- Hear—use a calming, relaxing, or uplifting sound/song
- Touch—use a soothing, comforting texture to relax you

Using Improve the moment:

- **I** Imagery—imagine or view a pleasant image, memory, place
- **M** Meaning—look for the meaning underneath the emotion
- **P** Prayer—pray, meditate, give it to your Higher Power
- **R** Relaxation—enjoy a relaxing activity (bubble bath, walk, nap)
- **O** One thing at a time—focus on One Thing and let the rest go
- **V** Vacation—take a mini-vacation (walk, coffee break)
- **E** Encouragement—be your own cheerleader—encourage yourself!

Distress Tolerance Skills

Distraction (A.C.C.E.P.T.S.)

Negative feelings will usually pass, or at least lessen in intensity over time. It can be valuable to distract yourself until the emotions subside. The acronym "A.C.C.E.P.T.S." serves as a reminder of this idea.

Activities	Engage in activities that require thought and concentration. This could be a hobby, a project, work, or school.
Contributing	Focus on someone or something other than yourself. You can volunteer, do a good deed, or do anything else that will contribute to a cause or person.
Comparisons	Look at your situation in comparison to something worse. Remember a time you were in more pain, or when someone else was going through something more difficult.
Emotions	Do something that will create a competing emotion. Feeling sad? Watch a funny movie. Feeling nervous? Listen to soothing music.
Pushing Away	Do away with negative thoughts by pushing them out of your mind. Imagine writing your problem on a piece of paper, crumbling it up, and throwing it away. Refuse to think about the situation until a better time.
Thoughts	When your emotions take over, try to focus on your thoughts. Count to 10, recite a poem in your head, or read a book.
Sensations	Find safe physical sensations to distract you from intense negative emotions. Wear a rubber band and snap it on your wrist, hold an ice cube in your hand, or eat something sour like a lime.

TherapistAid.com © 2015

Retrieved from: www.therapistaid.com

References & Recommended Reading

Clark, G. (2015). Mindfully Eating a Raisin. Retrieved August 5, 2015, from http://www.mbsrtraining.com/mindfully-eating-a-raisin-exercise/

Kennard, Deborah. (2015). EMDR Basic Training S.A.F.E. Approach. Personal Transformation Institute.

Linehan M. (1993). *Cognitive-behavioral treatment of borderline personality disorder.* New York: Guilford Press.

Linehan, Marsha. (2015). *DBT Skills Training Manual, 2nd ed*, The Guilford Press, New York, NY.

Merriam-Webster's collegiate dictionary (10th ed.). (1999). Springfield, MA: Merriam-Webster Incorporated.

National Association for Play Therapy: http://www.a4pt.org/

Rogers, Carl. (1995). *Client-Centered Therapy: Its Current Practice, Implications, and Theory.* Originally printed in 1980. Houghton-Mifflin, Boston: MA.

Rogers, Carl. (1980). *In A Way of Being.* Houghton-Mifflin, Boston: MA.

Rogers, Carl. (1931). *Measuring Personality Adjustment in Children Nine to Thirteen Years of Age.* Teacher's College, Columbia University: New York City, NY.

Rogers, Carl. (1939). *The Clinical Treatment of the Problem Child.* Houghton-Mifflin, Boston: MA.

Rogers, Carl. (1995). *Client-Centered Therapy: Its Current Practice, Implications, and Theory.* Originally printed in 1980. Houghton-Mifflin, Boston: MA.

Rogers, Carl. (1980). *In A Way of Being.* Houghton-Mifflin, Boston: MA.

Shapiro, Francine. (2018). *Eye Movement Desensitization and Reprocessing [EMDR] Therapy, 3rd ed.: Basic Principles, Protocols, and Procedures*. New York, The Guilford Press.

The Society of Clinical Child and Adolescent Psychology (2018)

Retrieved from: https://effectivechildtherapy.org/therapies/

About the Author:

The author, Dr. Kristi Godwin, is a South Georgia native who began writing at age nine. She was first published at age 12, won several writing awards as a child, and published her first anthology at age 17. She is an avid reader who loves to learn and explore a variety of subjects, and earned degrees in Psychology, Marriage and Family Therapy, and Public Administration in her adulthood. She also is passionate about human rights and the ethical treatment of animals, and has been an activist in both areas throughout her life. She founded a non-profit organization in 2008 geared toward inner-city, at-risk youth, and worked as a licensed therapist with troubled children and youth for over a decade.

Dr. Godwin is also the mother of four children and resides with her children and pets in Georgia. She currently works as a therapist with women who have a history of trauma. Works by Dr. Godwin include: A Collection of Poems, Words of Faith, White Anti-Racist Role Models, The Second Industrial Revolution Is Upon Us: The Future of Managing Human Resources in Public Administration (an anthology), Memoirs of a Southern Girl: The Story of My Life, Yea, Though I Walk…, Healing Beyond Trauma, God's Country, and A New Season of Poetry.

Find Dr. Godwin on Amazon and follow her Author Page to be notified of her new publications. For personal inquiries on how to address your own trauma or abuse history you may email her at: drkristibgodwin.author@yahoo.com.

Author Blog Page: www.BeTheAuthorOfYourLifeBook.blogspot.com

Author Facebook Page: www.facebook.com/BeTheAuthorOfYourLifeBook/

Related Training

- Trauma Informed Care 2-day workshop, Turning Point Hospital, Moultrie, GA April 2016
- EMDR Training, Tallahassee, FL, February 9-11, 2018 and March 9-11, 2018
- *Dialectical Behavior Therapy 2-Day Workshop, Americus Behavioral Health,* Connie Callahan, Ph.D., June 15-16, 2012.
- *Play Therapy and Beyond: Treatment Techniques and Strategies with Children and Pre-Adolescents, Steve* Green, Ph.D... Cross Country Education, February 2009.
- *Understanding the Impact of Trauma on Children,* University of Georgia School of Social Work, February 16, 2012.
- *Executive Dysfunction: The Disorganized, Defiant, and Chaotic Child/Adolescent,* Laura Ehlert, Ph.D., Americus Behavioral Health, May 30, 2012.
- *Resolving Trauma Without Drama,* Bill O Hanlon, MS, LMFT, Premier Education Solutions, Inc., Webstudy, December 2013.
- *Alcohol and the Family,* Department of Human Resources, January 21, 2009.
- *Bipolar Disorder in Children and Adolescents,* Department of Human Resources, January 20, 2009.
- *Suicide Prevention,* Department of Human Resources, January 20, 2009, and Turning Point Hospital, 2018.
- *Depressive Disorder in Children and Adolescents,* Department of Human Resources, May 26, 2009.
- *Abuse, Neglect, and Incident Reporting,* Department of Human Resources, May 26, 2009.

Made in the USA
Monee, IL
06 September 2021